•••• BULLETPOINTS •••

KU-417-300

OCEANS & RIVERS

John Farndon
Consultant: Peter Riley

Miles Kelly
PUBLISHING

First published by Miles Kelly Publishing Ltd
Bardfield Centre, Great Bardfield
Essex, CM7 4SL

ght © 2004 Miles Kelly Publishing
ok first appeared in *1000 Things You Should Know*

2 4 6 8 10 9 7 5 3 1

Editor: Isla MacCuish

Design: WhiteLight

ure Research: Liberty Newton

Production: Estela Godoy

British Library Cataloguing-in-Publication Data
A catalogue record for this book is available from the British Library

ISBN 1-84236-373-5

Printed in China

www.mileskelly.net
info@mileskelly.net

The publishers would like to thank the following artists who have contributed to this book:
Gary Hincks, Janos Marffy, Guy Smith

The publishers would also like to thank the following source for the use of their photograph:
Page 38 Ralph White/CORBIS

Contents

Rivers

- **Rivers** are filled with water from rainfall running directly off the land, from melting snow or ice or from a spring bubbling out water that is soaked into the ground.

- **High up in mountains** near their source (start), rivers are usually small. They tumble over rocks through narrow valleys which they carved out over thousands of years.

▲ *A river typically tumbles over boulders high up near its source.*

- **All the rivers** in a certain area, called a catchment area, flow down to join each other, like branches on a tree. The branches are called tributaries. The bigger the river, the more tributaries it is likely to have.

- **As rivers flow downhill,** they are joined by tributaries and grow bigger. They often flow in smooth channels made not of big rocks but of fine debris washed down from higher up. River valleys are wider and gentler lower down, and the river may wind across the valley floor.

- **In its lower reaches** a river is often wide and deep. It winds back and forth in meanders across broad floodplains made of silt from higher up.

- **Rivers flow fast** over rapids in their upper reaches. On average, they flow as fast in the lower reaches where the channel is smoother because there is much less turbulence.

- **Rivers wear away** their banks and beds, mainly by battering them with bits of gravel and sand and by the sheer force of the moving water.

- **Every river** carries sediment, which consists of large stones rolled along the river-bed, sand bounced along the bed and fine silt that floats in the water.

- **The discharge of a river** is the amount of water flowing past a particular point each second.

- **Rivers that flow** only after heavy rainstorms are 'intermittent'. Rivers that flow all year round are 'perennial' – they are kept going between rains by water flowing from underground.

In its upper reaches, a river tumbles over rocks through steep valleys

▼ *Some of the ways in which a river changes as it flows from its source high up in the hills downwards to the sea.*

The neck of a meander may in time be worn through to leave an oxbow lake

In its lower reaches, a river winds broadly and smoothly across flat floodplains

In its middle reaches, a river winds through broad valleys

Over flat land, a river may split into branches

5

River channels

- **A channel** is the long trough along which a river flows.

- **When a river's channel** winds or has a rough bed, friction slows the river down.

- **A river flows faster** through a narrow, deep channel than a wide, shallow one because there is less friction.

- **All river channels** tend to wind, and the nearer they are to sea level, the more they wind. They form remarkably regular horseshoe-shaped bends called meanders.

- **Meanders** seem to develop because of the way in which a river erodes and deposits sediments.

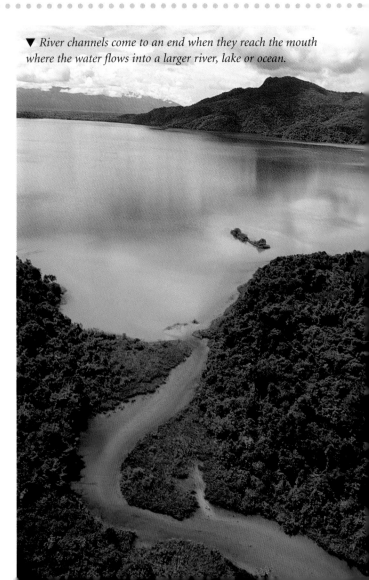

▼ *River channels come to an end when they reach the mouth where the water flows into a larger river, lake or ocean.*

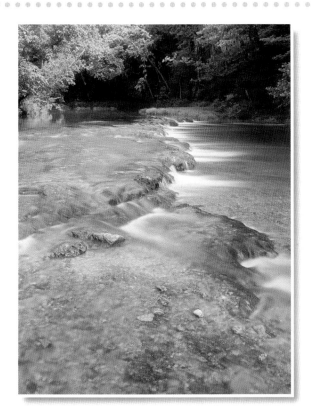

▲ *The river here is so wide and flat, and its bed so rough, that the water's flow is slowed by friction.*

...FASCINATING FACT...
Meanders can form almost complete loops
with only a neck of land separating the ends.

- **One key factor** in meanders is the ups and downs along the river called pools (deeps) and riffles (shallows).

- **The distance between pools and riffles,** and the size of meanders, are in close proportion to the river's width.

- **Another key factor** in meanders is the tendency of river water to flow not only straight downstream but also across the channel. Water spirals through the channel in a corkscrew fashion called helicoidal flow.

- **Helicoidal flow** makes water flow faster on the outside of bends, wearing away the bank. It flows more slowly on the inside, building up deposits called slip-off slopes.

River valleys

- **Rivers** carve out valleys as they wear away their channels.

- **High up in the mountains,** much of a river's energy goes into carving into the river-bed. The valleys there are deep, with steep sides.

- **Down** towards the sea, more of a river's erosive energy goes into wearing away its banks. It carves out a broader valley as it winds back and forth.

- **Large meanders** normally develop only when a river is crossing broad plains in its lower reaches.

- **Incised meanders** are meanders carved into deep valleys. The meanders formed when the river was flowing across a low plain. The plain was lifted up and the river cut down into it, keeping its meanders.

- **The Grand Canyon** is made of incised meanders. They were created as the Colorado River cut into the Colorado Plateau after it was uplifted 17 million years ago.

- **The shape of a river valley** depends partly on the structure of the rocks over which it is flowing.

◄ *Snake-like bends in a river's course are called meanders. They are often only separated by a narrow strip of land.*

▲ *Rivers carve out valleys over hundreds of thousands of years as they grind material along their beds.*

- **Some valleys** seem far too big for their river alone to have carved them. Such a river is 'underfit', or 'misfit'.

- **Many large valleys** with misfit rivers were carved out by glaciers or glacial meltwaters.

- **The world's rivers** wear the entire land surface down by an average of 8 cm every 1000 years.

Seas

- **Seas** are small oceans, completely enclosed or partly enclosed by land.

- **Seas** are shallower than oceans and do not have any major currents flowing through them.

- **In the Mediterranean** and other seas, tides can set up a seiche – a standing wave that sloshes back and forth like a ripple running up and down a bath.

- **If the natural** wave cycle of a seiche is different from the ocean tides, the tides are cancelled out.

- **If the natural** wave cycle of a seiche is similar to the ocean tides, the tides are magnified.

- **Scientists thought that** the Mediterranean was a dry desert 6 million years ago. They believed it was 3000 m lower than it is today, and covered in salts.

▲ *The warm waters of the Mediterranean attract tourists to the coast of Spain.*

- **Recent evidence** from microfossils suggests that the Mediterranean was never completely dry.

- **Warm seas such as the Mediterranean** lose much more water by evaporation than they gain from rivers. So a current of water flows in steadily from the ocean.

- **Warm seas** lose so much water by evaporation that they are usually much saltier than the open ocean.

▼ *Waves in enclosed seas tend to be much smaller than those in the open ocean, because there is less space for them to develop.*

...FASCINATING FACT...
The Dead Sea is the lowest sea on Earth,
400 m below sea level.

Pacific Ocean

- **The Pacific** is the world's largest ocean. It is twice as large as the Atlantic and covers over one third of the world, with an area of 181 million sq km.

- **It is over 24,000 km** across from Panama to the Malay Peninsula – more than halfway round the world.

- **The word 'pacific'** means calm. The ocean got its name from the 16th-century Portuguese explorer Magellan who was lucky enough to find gentle winds.

- **The Pacific is dotted** with thousands of islands. Some are the peaks of undersea volcanoes. Others are coral reefs sitting on top of the peaks.

▲ *There are thousands of of low lying islands in the Pacific. Most are only about a metre above sea level.*

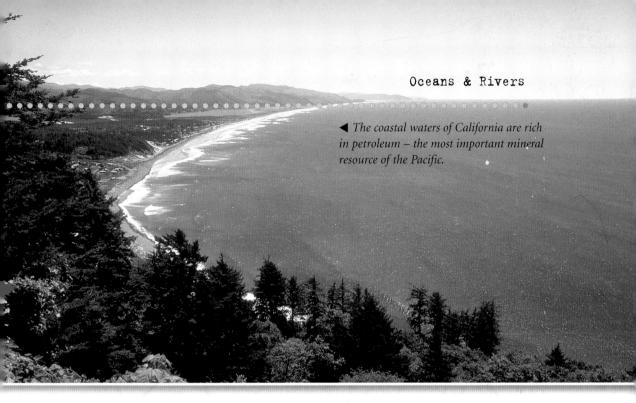

◄ *The coastal waters of California are rich in petroleum – the most important mineral resource of the Pacific.*

- **The Pacific** has some of the greatest tides in the world (over 9 m off Korea). Its smallest tide (just 0.3 m) is on Midway Island in the middle of the Pacific.

- **On average,** the Pacific Ocean is 4200 m deep.

- **Around the rim** there are deep ocean trenches including the world's deepest, the Mariana Trench.

- **A huge** undersea mountain range called the East Pacific Rise stretches from Antarctica up to Mexico.

- **The floor of the Pacific** is spreading along the East Pacific Rise at the rate of 12–16 cm per year.

- **The Pacific** has more seamounts (undersea mountains) than any other ocean.

13

Atlantic Ocean

▲ *The damp, cool climate of the northern Atlantic frequently turns its waters steely grey.*

- **The Atlantic Ocean** is the world's second largest ocean, with an area of 82 million sq km. It covers about one-fifth of the world's surface.

- **At its widest point,** between Spain and Mexico, the Atlantic is 9600 km across.

- **The Atlantic** was named by the ancient Romans after the Atlas Mountains of North Africa.

- **There are very few islands** in the main part of the Atlantic Ocean. Most lie close to the continents.

- **On average,** the Atlantic is about 3660 m deep.

- **The deepest point** in the Atlantic is the Puerto Rico Trench off Puerto Rico, which is 8648 m deep.

- **The Mid-Atlantic Ridge** is a great undersea ridge which splits the sea-bed in half. Along this ridge, the Atlantic is growing wider by 2–4 cm every year.

- **Islands** in the mid-Atlantic are volcanoes that lie along the Mid-Atlantic Ridge, such as the Azores and Ascension Island.

- **The Sargasso Sea** is a huge area of water in the western Atlantic. It is famous for its floating seaweed.

- **The Atlantic** is a youngish ocean, about 150 million years old.

▲ *The Atlantic Ocean provides around a quarter of the world's catch of fish.*

15

Indian Ocean

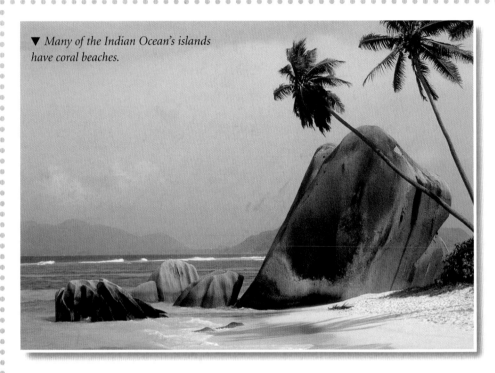

▼ *Many of the Indian Ocean's islands have coral beaches.*

- **The Indian Ocean** is the third largest ocean. It is about half the size of the Pacific Ocean and covers one-fifth of the world's ocean area. It has a total area of 73,426,000 sq km.

- **The average depth** of the Indian Ocean is 3890 m.

- **The deepest point** is the Java Trench off Java, in Indonesia, which is 7450 m deep. It marks the line where the Australian plate is being subducted under the Eurasian plate.

- **The Indian Ocean** is 10,000 km across at its widest point, between Africa and Australia.

- **Scientists believe** that the Indian Ocean began to form about 200 million years ago when Australia broke away from Africa, followed by India.

- **The Indian Ocean** is getting 20 cm wider every year.

- **The Indian Ocean** is scattered with thousands of tropical islands such as the Seychelles and Maldives.

- **The Maldives** are so low lying that they may be swamped if global warming melts the polar ice.

- **Unlike in other oceans,** currents in the Indian Ocean change course twice a year. They are blown by monsoon winds towards Africa in winter, and then in the other direction towards India in summer.

- **The Persian Gulf** is the warmest sea in the world; the Red Sea is the saltiest.

▶ *In the warm waters of the Indian Ocean coral reefs flourish.*

17

Arctic Ocean

▲ *Icebreakers are able to smash their way through sea ice using the strength of their reinforced bows.*

- **Most of the Arctic Ocean** is permanently covered with a vast floating raft of sea ice.

- **Temperatures** are low all year round, averaging -30°C in winter and sometimes dropping to -70°C.

- **During the long winters,** which last more than four months, the Sun never rises above the horizon.

- **The Arctic** gets its name from arctos, the Greek word for 'bear', because the Great Bear constellation is above the North Pole.

- **There are three kinds of sea ice** in the Arctic: polar ice, pack ice and fast ice.

- **Polar ice** is the raft of ice that never melts through.

- **Polar ice** may be as thin as 2 m in places in summer, but in winter it is up to 50 m thick.

- **Pack ice** forms around the edge of the polar ice and only freezes completely in winter.

- **The ocean swell** breaks and crushes the pack ice into chunky ice blocks and fantastic ice sculptures.

- **Fast ice** forms in winter between pack ice and the land around the Arctic Ocean. It gets its name because it is held fast to the shore. It cannot move up and down with the ocean as the pack ice does.

▲ *The seal is one of the few creatures that can survive the bitter cold of the Arctic winter.*

Southern Ocean

- **The Southern Ocean** is the world's fourth largest ocean. It stretches all the way round Antarctica, and has an area of 35,000,000 sq km.

- **It is the only ocean** that stretches all around the world.

- **In winter** over half the Southern Ocean is covered with ice and icebergs that break off the Antarctic ice sheet.

- **The East Wind Drift** is a current that flows anticlockwise around Antarctica close to the coast.

- **Further out** from the coast of Antarctica, the Antarctic circumpolar current flows in the opposite direction – clockwise from west to east.

- **The circumpolar current** carries more water than any other current in the world.

▲ *Many penguins such as the emperor, the world's largest penguin, live on the ice floes of the Southern Ocean.*

▲ *Beneath the surface of the Antarctic ice, the sea temperature reaches just -2°C. The freezing water is also a rich source of krill – tiny shrimp-like creatures.*

····FASCINATING FACT····
The circumpolar current could fill the Great Lakes in North America in just 48 hours.

- **The 'Roaring Forties'** is the band between 40° and 50° South latitude. Within this band strong westerly winds blow unobstructed around the world.

- **The waves in the 'Roaring Forties'** are the biggest in the world, sometimes higher than a ten-storey building.

- **Sea ice** forms in round pieces called pancake ice.

21

Beaches

- **Beaches** are sloping bands of sand, shingle or pebbles along the edge of a sea or lake.

- **Some beaches** are made entirely of broken coral or shells.

- **On a steep beach,** the backwash after each wave is strong. It washes material down the beach and so makes the beach gentler sloping.

- **On a gently sloping beach,** each wave runs in powerfully and falls back gently. Material gets washed up the beach, making it steeper.

> .... FASCINATING FACT ....
> The world's largest pleasure beach is Virginia Beach, Virginia, USA, over 45 km long.

▶ *Waves crashing against the shore can weaken cliffs and cause some to fall into the sea.*

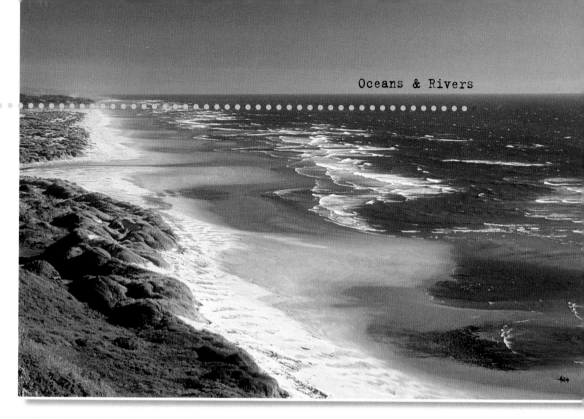

▲ *The little bays in this beach have been scooped out as waves strike the beach at an angle.*

- **The slope of a beach** matches the waves, so the slope is often gentler in winter when the waves are stronger.

- **A storm beach** is a ridge of gravel and pebbles flung high above the normal high-tide mark during a storm.

- **At the top of each beach** a ridge, or berm, is often left at the high-tide mark.

- **Beach cusps** are tiny bays in the sand that are scooped out along the beach when waves strike it at an angle.

- **Many scientists** believe that beaches are only a temporary phenomenon caused by the changes in sea levels after the last ice age.

Coasts

- **Coastlines** are changing all the time as new waves roll in and out and tides rise and fall every six hours or so. Over longer periods coastlines are reshaped by the action of waves and the corrosion of salty water.

- **On exposed coasts** where waves strike the high rocks, they undercut the slope to create steep cliffs and headlands. Often waves can penetrate into the cliff to open up sea caves or blast through arches. When a sea arch collapses, it leaves behind tall pillars called stacks which may be worn away to stumps.

- **Waves work** on rocks in two ways. First, the rocks are pounded with a huge weight of water filled with stones. Second, the waves force air into cracks in the rocks with such force that the rocks split apart.

- **The erosive power** of waves is focused in a narrow band at wave height. So as waves wear away sea cliffs, they leave the rock below wave height untouched. As cliffs retreat, the waves slice away a broad shelf of rock called a wave-cut platform. Water left behind in dips when the tide falls forms rockpools.

- **On more sheltered coasts,** the sea may pile up sand into beaches. The sand has been washed down by rivers or worn away from cliffs.

- **When waves hit** a beach at an angle, they fall straight back down the beach at a right angle. Any sand and shingle that the waves carry fall back slightly farther along the beach. In this way sand and shingle are moved along the beach in a zig-zag fashion. This is called longshore drift.

- **On beaches** prone to longshore drift, low fences called groynes are often built to stop the sand being washed away along the beach.

- **Longshore drift** can wash sand out across bays and estuaries to create sand bars called spits.

- **Bays** are broad indents in the coast with a headland on each side. Waves reach the headlands first, focusing their energy here. Material is worn away from the headlands and washed into the bay, forming a bay-head beach.

- **A cove is a small bay.** A bight is a huge bay, such as the Great Australian Bight. A gulf is a long narrow bight. The world's biggest bay is Hudson Bay, Canada, which has a shoreline 12,268 km long. The Bay of Bengal in India is larger in area.

▼ *The main features of a coastline.*

Wave-cut platform   Stack   Bay   Arch   Groyne   Spit

Waves

- **Waves in the sea** are formed when wind blows across the sea and whips the surface into ripples.

- **Water particles** are dragged a short way by the friction between air and water, which is known as wind stress.

- **If the wind continues to blow** long and strong enough in the same direction, moving particles may build up into a ridge of water. At first this is a ripple, then a wave.

- **Waves seem to move** but the water in them stays in the same place, rolling around like rollers on a conveyor belt.

- **The size of a wave** depends on the strength of the wind and how far it blows over the water (the fetch).

26

▲ *When waves enter shallow water, the water in them piles up until eventually they spill over at the top and break.*

...FASCINATING FACT...
A wave over 40 m high was recorded by the USS *Ramapo* in the Pacific in 1933.

- **If the fetch is short,** the waves may simply be a chaotic, choppy 'sea'. If the fetch is long, they may develop into a series of rolling waves called a swell.

- **One in 300,000 waves** is four times bigger than the rest.

- **The biggest waves** occur south of South Africa.

- **When waves** move into shallow water, the rolling of the water is impeded by the sea-bed. The water piles up, then spills over in a breaker.

27

Tsunamis

- **Tsunamis** are huge waves that begin when the sea floor is violently shaken by an earthquake, a landslide or a volcanic eruption.

- **In deep water** tsunamis travel almost unnoticeably below the surface. However, once they reach shallow coastal waters they rear up into waves 30 m high or higher.

- **Tsunamis** are often mistakenly called 'tidal waves', but they are nothing to do with tides. The word tsunami (soon-army) is Japanese for 'harbour wave'.

- **Tsunamis** usually come in a series of a dozen or more – anything from five minutes to one hour apart.

▼ *Tsunamis do little damage in open water but can cause huge amounts of damage in shallow waters and inland.*

A shift in the sea-bed sends
out a pulse of water

As the pulse moves into shallow
water it rears into a giant wave

▲ *Tsunamis may be generated underwater by an earthquake, then travel far along the sea-bed before emerging to swamp a coast.*

- **Before a tsunami arrives,** the sea may recede dramatically, like water draining from a bath.

- **Tsunamis can travel** along the sea-bed as fast as a jet plane, at 700 km/h or more.

- **Tsunamis** arrive within 15 minutes from a local quake.

- **A tsunami** generated by an earthquake in Japan might swamp San Francisco, USA, 10 hours later.

- **The biggest tsunami** ever recorded was an 85-m high wave which struck Japan on April 24, 1771.

- **Tsunami warnings** are issued by the Pacific Tsunami Warning Centre in Honolulu.

Tides

- **Tides are the way** the sea rises a little then falls back every 12 hours or so.

- **When the tide is flowing** it is rising. When the tide is ebbing it is falling.

- **Tides are caused** by the pull of gravity between the Earth, Moon and Sun.

- **The mutual pull** of the Moon's and the Earth's gravity stretches the Earth into an egg shape.

- **The solid Earth** is so rigid that it stretches only 20 cm.

- **Ocean waters** can flow freely over the Earth to create two tidal bulges (high tides) of water. One bulge is directly under the Moon, the other is on the far side of the Earth.

High tides happen at the same time each day on opposite sides of the Earth

▼ *At high tide, the sea rises up the shore and dumps seaweed, shells and drift wood. Most coasts have two high tides and two low tides every day.*

At high tide the water level rises

At low tide the water level goes down again

30

- **As the Earth rotates** every 24 hours the tidal bulges stay in the same place under the Moon. Each place on the ocean has high tide twice a day. The Moon is moving as well as the Earth, making high tides occur not once every 12 hours but once every 12 hours 25 minutes.

- **The continents** get in the way, making the tidal bulges slosh about in a complex way. As a result the timing and height of tides vary enormously. In the open ocean tides rise only 1 m or so, but in enclosed spaces such as the Bay of Fundy, in Nova Scotia, Canada they rise over 15 m.

- **The Sun is much farther away** than the Moon, but it is so big that its gravity has an effect on the tides.

- **The Moon and the Sun** line up at a Full and a New Moon, creating high spring tides twice a month. When the Moon and Sun pull at right angles at a Half Moon, they cause neap tides which are lower than normal tides.

▶ *Neap tides occur when the Sun and Moon are at right angles to each other and pulling in different directions.*

▶ *Spring tides occur when the Sun and the Moon are lined up and pulling together.*

31

Ocean currents

▲ *Ocean currents start as wind blows across the water's surface.*

- **Ocean surface currents** are like giant rivers, often tens of kilometres wide, 100 m deep and flowing at 15 km/h.

- **The major currents** are split on either side of the Equator into giant rings called gyres.

- **In the Northern Hemisphere** the gyres flow round clockwise; in the south they flow anticlockwise.

- **Ocean currents** are driven by a combination of winds and the Earth's rotation.

- **Near the Equator** water is driven by easterly winds to make westward-flowing equatorial currents.

- **When equatorial currents** reach continents, the Earth's rotation deflects them polewards as warm currents.

- **As warm currents flow** polewards, westerly winds drive them east back across the oceans. When the currents reach the far side, they begin to flow towards the Equator along the west coasts of continents as cool currents.

- **The North Atlantic Drift** brings so much warm water from the Caribbean to SW England that it is warm enough to grow palm trees, yet it is as far north as Newfoundland.

- **By drying out the air** cool currents can create deserts, such as California's Baja and Chile's Atacama deserts.

Wave movement

Surface currents

Underwater currents

▶ *The wind sets the surface waters in motion as currents. Waves create swirling circular currents, while deeper currents run beneath the surface.*

...FASCINATING FACT...
The West Wind Drift around Antarctica moves 2000 times as much water as the Amazon.

Deep ocean currents

▲ *This satellite picture shows variations in ocean surface temperature.*

- **Ocean surface currents** affect only the top 100 m or so of the ocean. Deep currents involve the whole ocean.

- **Deep currents** are set in motion by differences in the density of sea water. They move only a few metres a day.

- **Most deep currents** are called thermohaline circulations because they depend on the water's temperature ('thermo') and salt content ('haline').

- **If seawater** is cold and salty, it is dense and sinks.

- **Typically, dense water** forms in the polar regions. Here the water is cold and weighed down by salt left behind when sea ice forms.

- **Dense polar water** sinks and spreads out towards the Equator deep below the surface.

- **Oceanographers** call dense water that sinks and starts deep ocean currents 'deep water'.

- **In the Northern Hemisphere** the main area for the formation of deep water is the North Atlantic.

- **Dense salty water** from the Mediterranean pours deep down very fast – 1 m per second – through the Straits of Gibraltar to add to the North Atlantic deep water.

- **There are three levels** in the ocean: the 'epilimnion' (the surface waters warmed by sunlight, up to 100–300 m down); the 'thermocline', where it becomes colder quickly with depth; and the 'hypolimnion', the bulk of deep, cold ocean water.

▲ *In the polar regions the waters become colder and saltier which makes them heavier. They sink and spread slowly toward the Equator.*

Ocean deeps

- **The oceans** are over 2000 m deep on average.

- **Along the edge** of the ocean is a ledge of land – the continental shelf. The average sea depth here is 130 m.

- **At the edge of the continental shelf** the sea-bed plunges thousands of metres steeply down the continental slope.

- **Underwater avalanches** roar down the continental slope at over 60 km/h. They carve out deep gashes called submarine canyons.

- **The gently** sloping foot of the continental slope is called the continental rise.

- **Beyond the continental rise** the ocean floor stretches out in a vast plain called the abyssal plain. It lies as deep as 5000 m below the water's surface.

▼ *Under the ocean there are mountains, plateaus, plains and trenches similar to those found on land.*

Continental shelf

Continental slope

- **The abyssal plain** is covered in a thick slime called ooze. It is made partly from volcanic ash and meteor dust and partly from the remains of sea creatures.

- **The abyssal plain** is dotted with huge mountains, thousands of metres high, called seamounts.

- **Flat-topped seamounts** are called guyots. They may be volcanoes that once projected above the surface.

- **The deepest places** in the ocean floor are ocean trenches – made when tectonic plates are driven down into the mantle. The Mariana Trench is 10,863 m deep.

Plain

Oceanic crust

Underwater volcano

Ocean ridge

Deep-sea trench

▲ *Huge numbers of sea creatures live in the pelagic zone – the surface waters of the open ocean beyond the continental shelf.*

37

Black smokers

▲ *Black smokers were first discovered less than 30 years ago.*

- **Black smokers** are natural chimneys on the sea-bed. They billow black fumes of hot gases and water.

- **Black smokers** are technically known as hydrothermal vents. They are volcanic features.

- **Black smokers** form along mid-ocean ridges where the tectonic plates are moving apart.

- **Black smokers** begin when seawater seeps through cracks in the sea floor. The water is heated by volcanic magma, and it dissolves minerals from the rock.

- **Once the water is superheated,** it spews from the vents in scalding, mineral-rich black plumes.

- **The plume cools** rapidly in the cold sea, leaving behind thick deposits of sulphur, iron, zinc and copper in tall, chimney-like vents.

- **The tallest vents** are 50 m high.

- **Water jetting** from black smokers can reach 662°C.

- **Smokers** are home to a community of organisms that thrive in the scalding waters and toxic chemicals. The organisms include giant clams and tube worms.

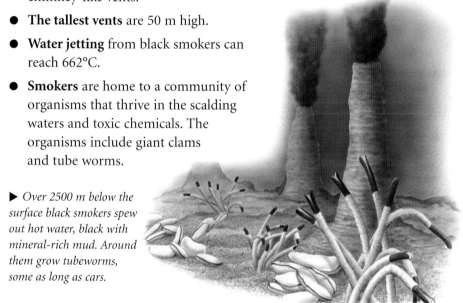

▶ *Over 2500 m below the surface black smokers spew out hot water, black with mineral-rich mud. Around them grow tubeworms, some as long as cars.*

FASCINATING FACT
Each drop of sea water in the world circulates through a smoker every ten million years.

39

Index